MAD®
MURDERS THE MOVIES

Written by
Dick De Bartolo

Illustrated by
Don Edwing

Edited by
Nick Meglin

WARNER BOOKS

A Warner Communications Company

DEDICATIONS

*To Dick De Bartolo, for providing the kind of rotten writing I can
save with my art!*

Don Edwing

*To Don Edwing, for providing the grotesque art that makes my
writing seem like classic literature!*

Dick De Bartolo

*To Dick De Bartolo and Don Edwing, for providing script and art
so inferior that it can make a lazy editor like me look like I'm
actually doing something constructive and creative!*

Nick Meglin

WARNER BOOKS EDITION

Title "MAD" used with permission of its owner, E.C. Publications, Inc.

This Warner Books Edition is published by arrangement with E.C. Publications, Inc.

Warner Books, Inc.
666 Fifth Avenue
New York, N.Y. 10103

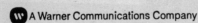 A Warner Communications Company

Printed in the United States of America

First Printing: July, 1985

10 9 8 7 6 5 4 3 2 1

Contents

OH, YES I WOULD...
'CAUSE FRANKLY STARLET,
I WON'T BUILD A DAM!
RRRRROAR!
DA-DUM-DEE DUM

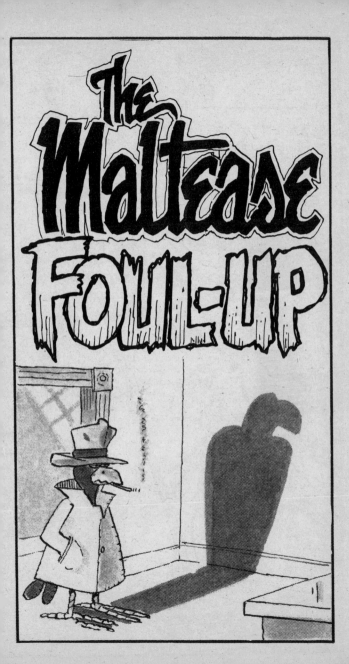

LET ME TELL YOU ABOUT THIS **SPECIAL STATUE** WE'RE TRYING TO RE-COVER!

IN 1539, THE KNIGHTS OF EMPEROR CHARLES NEEDED SOMETHING NICE TO PUT IN THE MIDDLE OF THEIR ROUND-TABLE, AND THEY ORDERED A **GOLDEN FALCON** CRESTED FROM HEAD-TO-FOOT IN DIAMONDS, RUBIES AND OTHER RARE GEMS! FOUR D-CELLS MADE IT GLOW FROM ACROSS THE ROOM-- IT WAS SPECTACULAR!

SINCE THE FALCON COST SO MUCH TO MAKE, THERE WAS ONLY ENOUGH MONEY LEFT FOR THE MANUFACTURER TO **MAIL** IT TO THE KNIGHTS. NATURALLY, IT **DISAPPEARED!** TWO HUNDRED YEARS LATER IT WAS RETURNED FOR **ADDITIONAL POSTAGE**, AND SENT OFF **AGAIN!** IT SURFACED IN A **DEAD LETTER OFFICE** IN SICILY TWO MONTHS AGO!

THE INSIDE IS ALL HARD STUF LIKE DIAMONDS AND JEWELS! YOU'D BREAK YOUR TEETH!
SO THROW IT OUT!
TO GALLOWS

MEANWHILE, BACK IN TOWN, FRANKENSHTICK'S FIANCE AND FRIENDS WORRY ABOUT FRANKENSHTICK...
I'LL SAY! EVER SINCE HE TOOK UP RESIDENCE IN THAT CREEPY CASTLE, HE'S BEEN ACTING WEIRD! HE ASKED FOR MY HAND IN MARRIAGE...
WHAT'S SO WEIRD ABOUT THAT?
HE SAID HE ONLY WANTED MY HAND! HE SAID HE HAD ENOUGH OTHER PARTS!

ROBBIN' CALLED HIS BAND 'THE MERRY MEN' BECAUSE THEY OFTEN DANCED WITH EACH OTHER AND CARRIED ON A LOT. THE TOWNS-PEOPLE CALLED THEM A LOT OF *OTHER* THINGS...

WANT TO SHOW YOU SOMETHING, MAD MARION! HESE ARE THE PEOPLE I HAVE BEEN HELPING! EVERY CENT I HAVE EVER STOLEN, I HAVE GIVEN TO THEM!
EVERY CENT YES, BUT HE KEEPS THE DOLLARS FOR HIMSELF!
IT'S NOT EASY LIVING IN THE TALLEST TREE IN CHEER-WOOD FOREST! I HAVE A HIGH OVERHEAD!

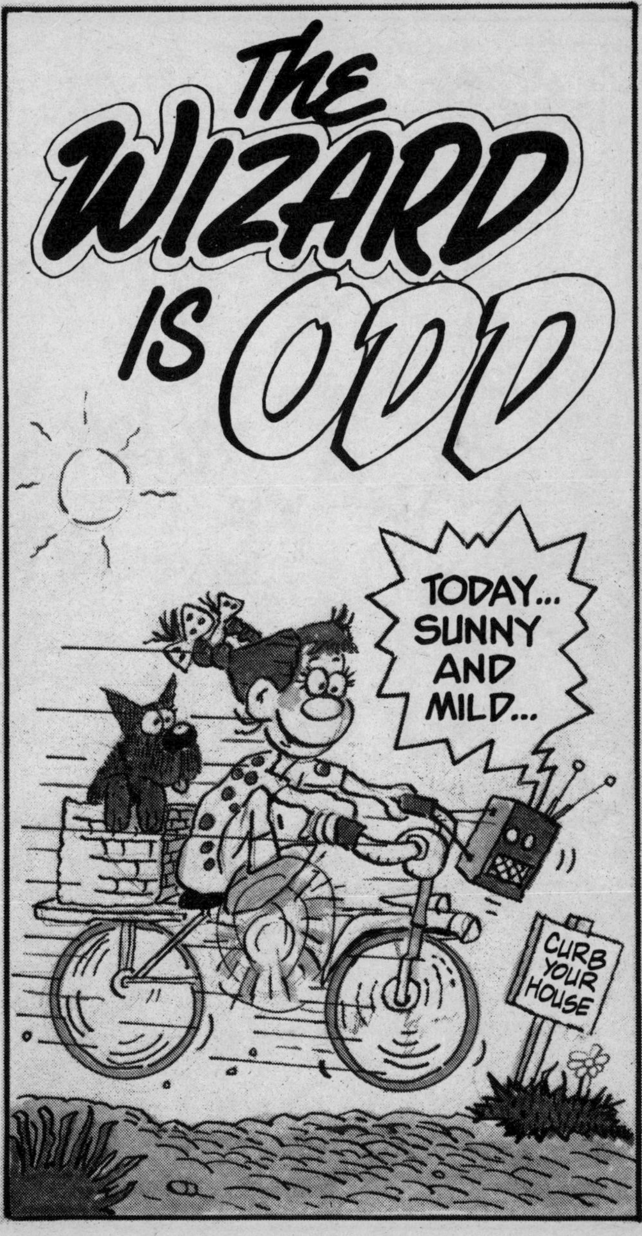
THE WIZARD IS ODD
TODAY... SUNNY AND MILD...
CURB YOUR HOUSE